MARINE LIFE

PUNCH
at Sea

Edited by William Hewison

A PUNCH BOOK
Published in Association with Grafton
An Imprint of HarperCollins*Publishers*

Grafton
An Imprint of HarperCollins*Publishers*
77–85 Fulham Palace Road
Hammersmith, London W6 8JB

Published by Grafton 1991
1 3 5 7 9 10 8 6 4 2

A catalogue record for this book
is available from the British Library

ISBN 0-586-21481-X

Printed in Great Britain by
Mackays of Chatham plc, Chatham, Kent

Introduction

All right, we all know of a certain Foundation whose grants have long been used on some fairly whacky projects, sending young American graduates hither and yon across the world in order to scratch away at some arcane piece of trivia and at the same time give the researcher a happy freebie in some foreign field, but are there still enough whacky projects at hand, awaiting the OK from that Foundation? Undoubtedly there are, and I can offer one such – good enough for a 20,000-word thesis and a stack of footnotes and appendices.

How about 'The Psychological Imperative of the Desert Island in Cartoon Creativity'?

As far as cartoon clichés are concerned, there are plenty of them lying around: yogis on beds of nails, the Ark, psychiatrists' couches, the Trojan horse, salesmen at the door, for instance – but time and time again the cartoonist, toiling to squeeze out his weekly quota of ideas, turns to that simple mound of sand in the ocean, that single palm tree, that solitary castaway. Why? On the face of it the subject would appear to be so restrictive, so bereft of creative basics, yet the notions still come shooting off the drawing boards until cartoon editors jump up and shout, 'Enough! No more desert islands!'

Unfortunately the next batch of offerings they look at will probably contain a spanking new twist to the desert island formula, a piece of inspired invention that forbids its rejection. I tell you, no budding cartoonist worth his salt feels he has properly passed his apprenticeship unless he has succeeded in getting a palmed atoll or two into the public prints.

But remember, cartoonists are a crafty lot, always nudging the boundaries outwards a bit, adding dimensions, introducing extra accoutrements to help things along; so a second castaway wades ashore, which permits games of cricket, two-party democratic states and time-warped conversation. If this second castaway turns out to be a woman then the scope jumps several notches.

All this is to explain why I have sneaked so many desert islands into this collection. They just demand to be there, especially if I include that secondary tropical island theme: Robinson Crusoe and the footprint. (That's practically another genus on its own.)

But, of course, this book sets its sights much wider than that; it is a salt-water navigation around the snorkelling bathers and family games on the seashore, the amateur yachtsmen (and women) floundering across the bay, the whiskery sea-dogs splicing the mainbrace on the high seas. It takes in ancient history (Phoenician galley-slaves oar-pulling to the beat of the drum) and ancient myth (Moses shoving the Red Sea apart). Maritime legend is acknowledged through the mystery of the abandoned *Marie Celeste* (and if that name means nothing to you them I'm afraid those gags will fall flat), and there are pirates, oil spillage and sea pollution, and lone yachtsmen sailing their sponsored vessels around the world. Cross-Channel swimmers are frequently noticed, but the real meaty stuff that gets our cartoonists grabbing at their biros is disaster at sea – the sinkings, the shipwrecks, the survivors clinging to the wreckage. If there is a classic cartoon devoted to this theme then it must be Spencer's drawing of two members of the ship's band floating on their cello-cases with one of them musing, 'I wonder how the piccolo player is making out.'

Finally, I cannot resist a 19th-century oldie – a John Leech drawing in its full cross-hatched and elaborately captioned glory. It, too, concerns a ship's orchestra, but its main attraction to me is in its first use of a caption cliché still around today: 'Why listen, darling, they're playing *our* tune.'

William Hewison

"We'll go home when the tide reaches that rock, O.K.?"

*"O.K., so we're sunburnt – **now** what?"*

"Ready or not – here I come!"

"Crew? Between the lot of them they only make up one whole pirate . . ."

"I think Henderson is crazed by thirst"

"It's our only concession to the World Wildlife Fund"

"Terrible news – the Golden Hind is back."

"Hold it! Harry's got cramp!"

"I remember one terrible night back in 'sixty-three, on the Exeter By-pass."

"I wonder how the piccolo player is making out."

"Actually we've managed rather well – baby-sitters have been a problem, of course ..."

"Oh dear, it's that dreadful Ramsbottom person."

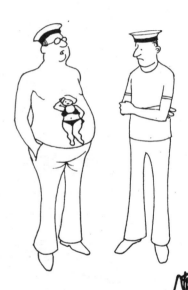

*"Of course, she was slim when
I first married her."*

"Any other man would have built a raft!"

thelwell

"Sawdust and shavings about all winter – and for what?"

"*I've never tried this one before.*"

"My pipe! My slippers!"

"I hate to leave him – he was developing into a useful leg-spinner."

"*Please, Hartley, remember our gentleman's agreement.*"

"The Missus and me used to run a cats' home – till an old dear left us fifty thousand in her will."

"Talk about undertow . . ."

"We're not overlooked here. We can be just as self-conscious as we want to be."

"Well, I feel we've proved the Micronesians didn't get to Tahiti from here!"

*"You thought hunger, thirst and loneliness had driven you insane but,
Eddie Leggit, 'This is Your Life'."*

"Ah well, some days you win and some days you lose!"

"No . . . I didn't hear anything!"

"Bingo!"

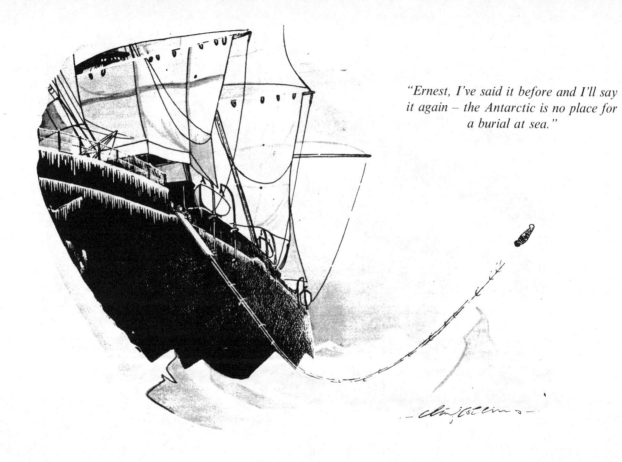

"Ernest, I've said it before and I'll say it again – the Antarctic is no place for a burial at sea."

"Thank goodness you saw my distress rocket!"

"What we now have to decide is – which of us has run out of food?"

" . . . and **I** could cut down palm trees and make us a cosy hut, and **you** could gather wild fruit and milk the goats . . . "

" . . . the Marie Celeste was a spy
ship . . . the Marie Celeste was . . . "

"He's not the white whale his father was."

"Permission to get the women and children into the lifeboats, Cap'n?"

"I suppose we've got a lot to be thankful for, really."

"I think the rules allow us to empty her bra round about now."

"All right, if it will humour you, there's my IOU for five hundred million pounds."

"He's been specially recommended by the Good Pirate Guide."

"Gabriella! Get below decks! This is no place for a woman."

" . . . So there I were in Marks and Spencer tryin' on the fishermen's jumpers
when, suddenly, I spied this half-price yachting cap . . . "

"Well, what category do you want to start off with today: show tunes, football or great names in American painting?"

"I've just discovered . . .

. . . this is the one place . . .

. . . I don't feel sea-sick."

"The tide is out at the moment, but if you'd care to leave your number at the end of this tone . . . "

"In the name of democracy, welcome! Up to now we've had a one-party system."

"Of course, when I were a lad, all this were minefields."

"Look right, look left . . . "

"You're out! Off-side!"

"No, Jim lad! That's my Sunday leg!"

"You realise what this is going to mean to 'Genesis'?"

"*The only thing we've got to watch out for is that hidden streak of non-violence in our national character.*"

"Hot? This? You should have been here **last** week."

"Hello! The cargo's shifted."

"I haven't seen another human being for fifty years, sir."

"Really, Henry! That's one drink you could cut down on!"

"Isn't it marvellous with the women and kids out of the way?"

"Shove off! You can't rescue me in Chapter Two!"

"If there's one thing I insist on – it's a happy ship."

"He is to beachcombing what Einstein is to physics."

"For God's sake, Gerald, unwind gradually!"

Angelina (to her beloved Edwin, as the ship's orchestra, in the saloon below, strikes up unexpectedly with "NEARER, MY GOD, TO THEE"): "WHY, LISTEN, DARLING, THEY'RE PLAYING OUR TUNE!"

"I've run out of blue."

"The compass is faulty, you're asleep, the crew's drunk, your radio's broken and the ship's running aground . . . whom do you blame?"

"Bless you, Nigel."

"Beg pardon."

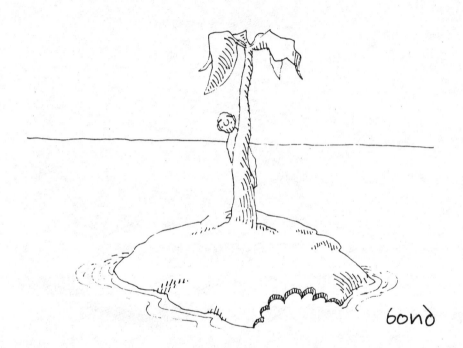

bond

"O for pity's sake let him light it!"

"Well, I say thank God for the misguided design sense of the managing director's mother."

"Just what the hell kind of Viking are you anyhow?"

"That's the crew all right but where's the Marie Celeste?"

"I'm sick to death of rabbit stew!"

"Hey!"

"I certainly wouldn't care to be in his shoes."

"The ship's cat won't touch tinned meat."

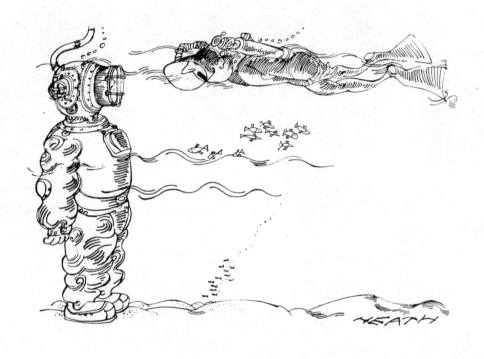

"Get with it, Benson. Nobody dresses like that any more."

*"Believe me, my young friend, there is **nothing** – absolutely nothing – half so expensive as simply messing about in boats!"*

"If anyone hears that engine we'll be ostracised at the club."

"It would have been enough to bless the fishing fleet."

*"I'm tired of these world cruises . . .
can't we go somewhere else?"*

"It's your turn to prune the bonsai."

"I thought there was a dock strike on here!"

"He's terribly shy. It was his turn to take off his shirt."

"Good Lord! Look at Madge Weston – he's old enough to be her husband!"

"I'm sorry mate. It's a single-handed race."

*"I don't see it matters a damn if we're flotsam **or** jetsam!"*

"What a waste, Harry, that this should happen to a man with your contacts."

"Jeez, what next? First a bleedin' earthquake and now a snowstorm."

*"It could have been a damned sight worse, eh, steward? Only **one** passenger to look after from now on."*

"*I've got an idea! We could take the same cruise again and go* **tourist***!*"

"As a matter of fact I've only been here since yesterday – I was appearing in the ship's pantomime."

"Attention all shipping!"

"Wouldn't it be easier to go back and get your reading glasses?"

"You risked your life for me, young man – you must let me sell you some insurance."

"It's such a nice day we've decided to stay on the beach."

"Write that the island is being over-run by communist agitators spreading anti-American propaganda and proving a serious threat to our democratic way of life – that ought to fetch them!"

"Hi, gorgeous!"

"He's got some story about a
fabulous land in the West."

"For God's sake bring a toothpick!"

"I expect there'll be another along in a minute."

"They're going on: the idiots must think we're on some damn-fool Atlantic crossing stunt."

"But on the other hand they act as a sail."

"Underground atomic tests don't help either."

"Please excuse scribble."

"First-class passengers always get the de luxe burial."

*"You're not bringing that oil on **this** beach."*

". . . and all who sail in her!"

"When you've been at sea as long as I have, Jenkins,
you'll know that an oil slick has many moods."

"Don't be ridiculous, Walter!"

"I'll try to lay on a band or something."

FEMALE
CONTORTIONIST
IN
VIEW

" The first thing you've got to do is get over feeling self-conscious."

*"Now **that's** what I call a good water-repellent raincoat!"*

"No, you can't have chicken for dinner – we've had it twice already."